# ELLA FITZGERALD

## The Tale of a Vocal Virtuosa

BY **ANDREA DAVIS PINKNEY**

WITH SCAT CAT MONROE

ILLUSTRATED BY **BRIAN PINKNEY**

 Jump at the Sun    Los Angeles ★ New York

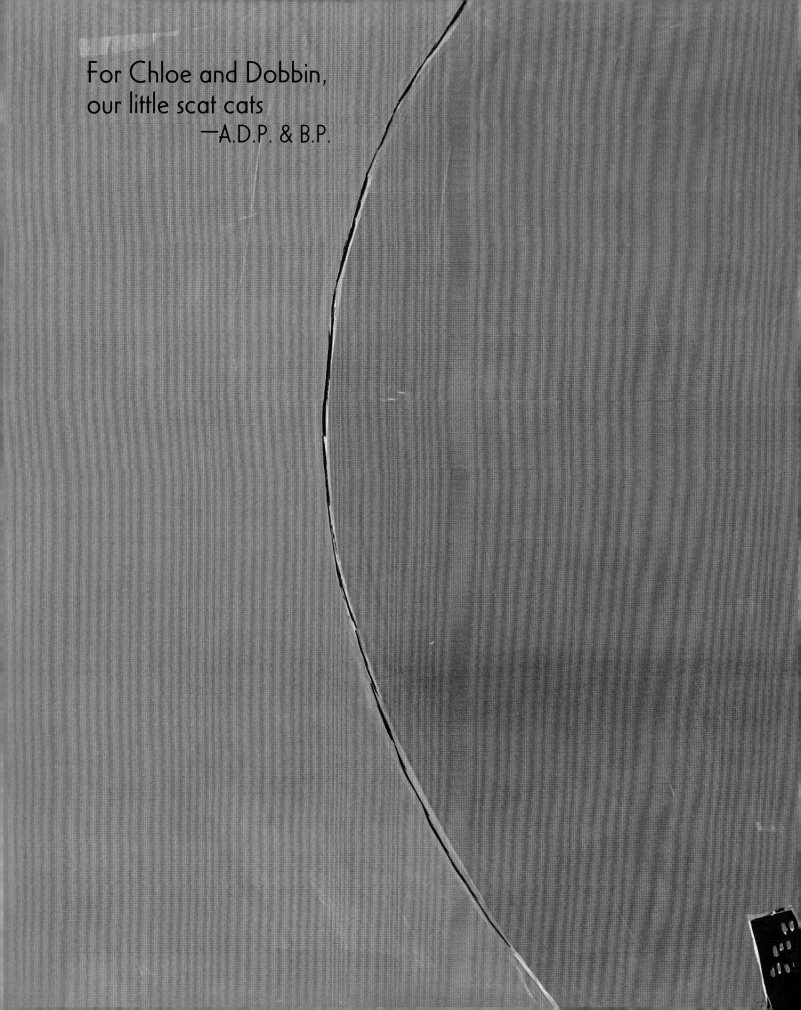

For Chloe and Dobbin,
our little scat cats
—A.D.P. & B.P.

**Y**ou may think I look like any other cat.

But, baby, I'm in a class all by myself.

Scat Cat's my name. Scat Cat Monroe.

A name I've earned.

Got my name from knowin' Ella.

Ella Fitzgerald. The Queen of Scat.

What's scat? you ask.

Scat's the sound that don't hold back.

*Ella's* sound—*that* was scat.

Singing so supreme.

Music's velvet-ribbon dream.

Let me tell you Ella's story.

'Cause, you see, I was there. From the get-go.

I saw it all. Me. Scat Cat Monroe.

I watched Ella go from a small-town girl to the First Lady of Song.

To a Vocal Virtuosa, bar none.

So, sit back. Listen up. Here's four tracks.

Cut to cut.

Here's how Ella got her sound.

Got her silken silver style.

Got her Lady Ella scat!

# Track 1
## Hoofin' in Harlem

The child's name was Ella. She was a big-boned girl with dreams of becoming a dancer. But there weren't many dance schools in Yonkers, New York, the little city where Ella Fitzgerald and her mother, Tempie, lived.

Ella had her heart set on pretty-steppin' her way to fame—and she didn't need a dance school to do it. She taught *herself* to tap-dance.

Determination was her teacher.

The sidewalk was her stage.

Imagination was her spotlight.

In time, Ella and her friends took to performing on street corners. When Ella's neighbors saw her go, they told Ella to strut her shuffle in Harlem. To take her hoofin' to New York—the big city—where dreams really *do* come true.

That's when Harlem became Ella's stomping ground. On the night of November 21, 1934, Ella entered a talent contest at the Apollo Theatre. She was seventeen, and scrubbed clean down to her toe jam. But as soon as Ella saw the footlights, her feet failed her.

She stood front and center.

Knees knockin'.

Teeth clackin'.

A wanna-be, with a stomach full of butterflies.

And the girl was hardly dressed to impress. She wore work boots and hand-me-downs.

Luckily, Ella was thinking on her toes. She refused to be booed back to Yonkers, so she started to sing. At first, her voice came quiet as a whisper. A measly little hiss, soft as a cricket. But when the band joined in, Ella rolled out a tune sweet enough to bake. She won the contest straight up, kicked her dance dreams to the curb, and pinned all her hopes on being a singer.

I was there in the wings, watching it all. Swinging to Ella's groove, wearing a grin as big and as proud as that Cheshire dude.

# Track 2
## Jammin' at Yale

Soon Ella had audiences eating out of her hand. She went on to win talent showcases all over
Harlem. In 1935, the Harlem Opera House signed her as a featured singer. One night,
Bardou Ali, the master of ceremonies for the Chick Webb Orchestra, saw Ella perform.

That's when Bardou knew. Knew that Chick needed Ella. And that Ella needed Chick. That
the two of them could make beautiful music together.

But you see, Chick was a finicky bird. Easy to ruffle. Hard to please. A perfectionist.

He was a jazz drummer who liked his music hot. Swing music was Chick's style, cut-the-rug
rhythms that put the pulse on a party. He believed folks came to hear the instruments in his
band, not some singer. Besides, he already had a singer for his orchestra, a guy named Charlie
Linton. What Chick didn't know was that Ella's voice was its own instrument.

When Bardou took Ella to meet Chick, Chick agreed to give Ella a chance. He told her she could sing with his orchestra at a college dance the next night. At Yale University—the *Ivy* League, where gettin' loose don't always come easy. Chick told Ella that if she could work that college crowd, she could join his band.

So Ella went to Yale with a purpose. And, man, once Ella started to sing, she had them Yalies *jammin'*.

That night, Chick welcomed Ella into his band. He took her under his wing, and the two of them flew to the Savoy Ballroom, the hippest dance spot in Harlem.

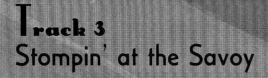

# Track 3
## Stompin' at the Savoy

The Chick Webb Orchestra had a regular gig at the Savoy. Night after night, they played to a house packed tighter than the A train. The place was crammed full of folks who'd come to shake their tails to the orchestra's sound.

And, honey, Yours Truly could shake with the best of them! You ever see a cat do the Kangaroo? The Lindy Hop? The Suzie Q? Those were the moves we danced at the Savoy. Danced while Ella belted from the bandstand. It was Chick's drumming that pulled people onto the dance floor. It was Ella's singing that kept them there.

Ella was not like other highfalutin singers. She never forgot where she came from. She remembered that her first work as a performer had been on the street.

After Ella sang, she stepped down from the stage and danced with her fans. Ella let them know she was one of them. She showed them she could Kangaroo, too. She stomped at the Savoy like any other paying customer.

Chick Webb was born with a beat in his bones. He was a master drummer. A musician with a fix on jazz. Ella made it her business to learn all she could from Chick. She had talent. He had know-how.

Chick showed Ella the right way to deliver a song. He taught her to shade the high notes and light the lows. To grab hold of a tune. To wrap her voice around each melody.

When the sun set on Harlem, and the cats and kitties came out to play, it was Ella and Chick they were coming to see. When Chick and Ella performed together, they were grits with gravy—they brought out the best in each other. People called it chemistry. I called it musical magic.

On May 11, 1937, the Chick Webb Orchestra took on the Benny Goodman Orchestra in the Savoy's battle of the bands. These contests were a Savoy tradition, and, child, they were *fierce*. One band tried to outplay the other, till the crowd—with their applause—named the winner.

Benny Goodman was called the "King of Swing." He played the clarinet. But King Benny didn't have Ella, who would someday be known as the queen of her craft. And he didn't have Chick Webb, a royal percussionist.

Benny set the contest in motion. His band started with a song called "Peckin'." They made the place swing, no doubt.

Then Chick's band took their turn. Chick's drum solos were *slammin'*. They backed up Ella's vocals, which gave new meaning to the word *divine*.

The contest was close from the get-go. Those musicians put a fever to the room. They had me sweatin' the sheen off my fur, and scuffin' my wing-tip shoes. When Chick's band played "Harlem Congo," the crowd got hotter than bootleg Tabasco. That's 'cause Ella set "Harlem Congo" on fire. Her voice was quick-fried rhythm, with a brassy satin twist.

She sizzled with Chick's cymbals.

Busted loose with his bongos.

She tamed the crowd while Chick played his timpani.

And, man, that ain't all!

Ella worked the downbeat. She *milked* the backbeat.

She sang like tomorrow wasn't ever gonna come.

Four thousand people filled the Savoy Ballroom that night. The contest lasted five hours. When it was done, everybody knew who was boss.

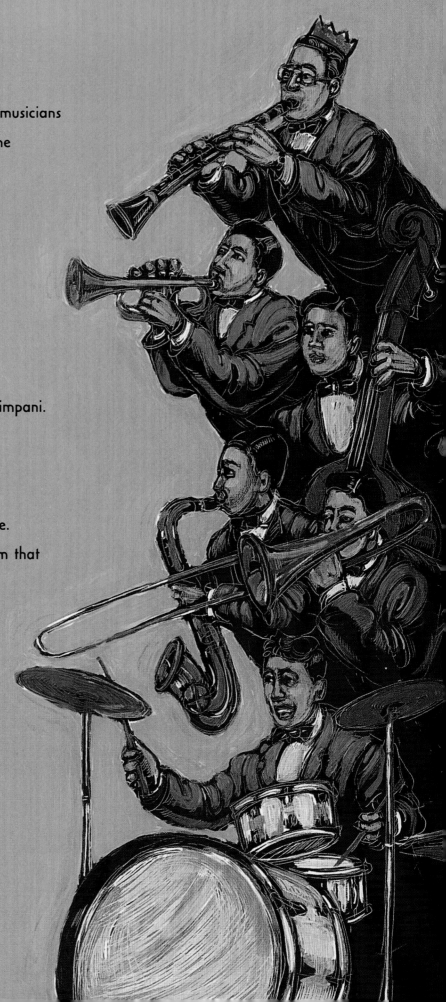

# Track 4
## Carnegie Hall Scat

The Savoy was Ella's stepping-stone. Thanks to nightly radio broadcasts from the club, *Ella* was the name sittin' pretty on everybody's lips.

Ella took the Chick Webb Orchestra to new heights. She was the orchestra's star attraction. Nightclub owners had to wait in line to book the band. Some of them had never had a black singer perform at their clubs. Ella's popularity showed them that a true star has no color—it just shines.

Ella could even put stardust in a ditty. In 1938, she and Al Feldman, a member of Chick's band, wrote and recorded "A-Tisket, A-Tasket."

Man, when you're an alley cat like me, you hear all kinds of hopscotch chatter and jump-rope jive. "A-Tisket, A-Tasket" wasn't nothin' more than a nursery rhyme, chanted a million times a day by kitties from Sugar Hill to Hollywood. But to hear Ella swing that brown-and-yellow basket was a whole 'nother thing. "A-Tisket, A-Tasket" was a smash hit. In time, folks came to call the song a jitterbug spiritual.

Ella didn't shy back from any kind of music. When bebop became hotter than swing jazz, and music lovers turned to Bird and Dizzy, Ella took her place on the bebop bandwagon.

Bebop was jazz on the wild side. It was:

## SYN-CO-PATION.
## LO-CO-MOTION.

Fast-smack sound—done low down.

It was *slam-bamming* on the *flitter-tip.*

It was *ham-hock-jabber.*

# FEVER. Pitch.

Dizzy Gillespie was bebop's main man. He turned jazz on its head. With his trumpet, he could blow notes into back flips. Into flatted fifths. Into popcorn blips that flung free from his horn. Dizzy asked Ella to join his band. He invited Ella to give bebop a try. To improvise. To sing the ping-pong rhythms that gave bebop its sound.

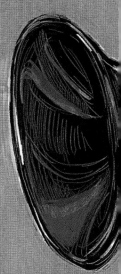

Ella went along for Dizzy's ride. One night, when the two of them started to jam, Ella made bebop her own. For Ella, scat singing drove bebop home. Ella used her voice in the same way Dizzy used the notes he made with his horn—like a runaway leaf flying high on a breeze.

Now, when Ella performed, she let her lyrics go. She took her singing out to play. When Ella recorded "How High the Moon," her scat swung to cloud nine and back.

On September 29, 1947, Ella and Dizzy headlined a sold-out performance at Carnegie Hall. They brought bebop to a high-and-mighty concert stage. But the show was far from uppity. It was *fun*.

Dizzy's trumpet chirped. It zipped. It sputtered in double-time tem

Dizzy bounced his be

's singing hung fast to Dizzy's rhythm.

lla.

Ella shot him back her scat.

Man, those two were making up music in the moment.
It was *invention*.
It was *frolic*.
It was *cooler than cool*.
Ella put scat on the map. When she and Dizzy threw down
their *skippity-hop-doo-dee-bop*, every soul in the place slipped
into the jam.

Ella soon had fans who loved all kinds of music. They came to call Ella by many names: The Queen of Scat. The First Lady of Song. A Vocal Virtuosa.

Now *I'm* the keeper of Ella's flame. The teller of her tale. The Scat Cat.

So kid, don't be fooled by phony felines. A cat by any other name ain't the same. Take it from me. Scat Cat Monroe. I was there. With Ella. From the get-go.

# A Note from the Author

Ella Jane Fitzgerald was born on April 25, 1917, in Newport News, Virginia.

She never knew her father, who separated from Ella's mother when she was a baby. Her mother, Tempie, died when Ella was a teenager. She spent the last years of her childhood living with relatives.

Soon after the death of her mother, Ella joined the Chick Webb Orchestra. Under Chick's tutelage, Ella's career took off.

Ella Fitzgerald is perhaps best known for her scat singing—abandoning the lyrics of a song to use nonsense syllables to carry the rhythm. Though trumpeter Louis Armstrong is said to have originated scat singing, it was Ella Fitzgerald who made scat popular.

Scatting was Ella's way of adapting her vocal style to bebop music, which, in the early 1940s, was emerging as a new kind of jazz.

In 1948 Ella joined "Jazz at the Philharmonic," a traveling tour of jazz musicians. Conceived by music promoter Norman Granz, the "Jazz at the Philharmonic" troupe was created, in part, to encourage racial harmony and to make jazz popular throughout the world. With Granz's leadership, the musicians on the tour played to integrated audiences. This was an uncommon phenomenon in the 1940s.

A few years later Norman Granz became Ella's manager. It was Granz who realized that Ella could reach a wider audience by recording the songs of popular American composers. Granz compiled the works of several greats—Irving Berlin, George and Ira Gershwin, Cole Porter—which Ella recorded for Verve, a record label owned by Granz.

During her lifetime, Ella's genius was rewarded with thirteen Grammy Awards, a Lifetime Achievement Award, and countless other musical citations.

In 1979 Ella was honored at Washington, D.C.'s Kennedy Center by President Jimmy Carter and First Lady Rosalynn Carter, who named Ella one of the most talented American performers who has ever lived. And, in 1987, President Ronald Reagan presented Ella with the National Medal of Arts to recognize her life's achievements.

Ella Fitzgerald has been referred to as the undying flame that lights our national music heritage. Even after her death on June 15, 1996, her brilliance has continued to shine.

—A.D.P.

# A Note from the Illustrator

To add visual authenticity to Ella Fitzgerald's story, I was inspired by the works of several Harlem Renaissance artists who were working when Ella Fitzgerald came of age in Harlem. One such artist was Aaron Douglas, who possessed an incredible design sensibility. Another artist of the period whose work I admire is William H. Johnson, who brought tremendous energy to his paintings and so beautifully depicted black people. The color palette of the Art Deco movement, which was in vogue during Ella's youth, also served as a bolt of inspiration as I told Ella's tale through pictures.

The paintings for this book were rendered in scratchboard—a white board that's covered with black ink, then scratched away to reveal the white underneath. Once the scratchboard drawings were complete, I then tinted them with transparent luma dyes and painted them with acrylics.

—B.P.

## Bibliography

Gillespie, Dizzy, with Al Fraser. *To Be or Not to Bop: Memoirs of Dizzy Gillespie.* New York: Da Capo Press, 1979.
Kliment, Bud. *Ella Fitzgerald: First Lady of American Song.* New York: Chelsea House Publishers, 1988.
*New Grove Dictionary of American Music, The.*
Nicholson, Stuart. *Ella Fitzgerald: A Biography.* New York: Charles Scribner's Sons, 1994.
Wyman, Carolyn. *Ella Fitzgerald: Singer Supreme.* New York: Franklin Watts, 1993.

## Videography

*Ella Fitzgerald: Something to Live For.* American Masters series. Public Broadcasting Service, 1999.
*Forever Ella.* ABC News Productions and A&E Television Networks, 1999.
*Jazz Classics—Harlem Harmonies,* vol. I. 1940–1945. Rahway, N.J.: Videofidelity, 1986.
*Jazz Classics—Harlem Harmonies,* vol. II. 1941–1946. Rahway, N.J.: Amvest Video, 1987.

## Selected Discography

*Ella Fitzgerald Sings the Cole Porter Songbook* (Verve Records).
*Ella Fitzgerald Sings the George and Ira Gershwin Songbook* (Verve Records).
*Ella in Berlin* (Verve Records).
*Ella Returns to Berlin* (Verve Records).
*Ella and Louis* (Verve Records).

Special thanks
to the Museum of the City of New York,
the Carnegie Hall Archives,
and especially to Quincy Troupe
for their research assistance